Curriculum Visions

Exploring ancient Rome

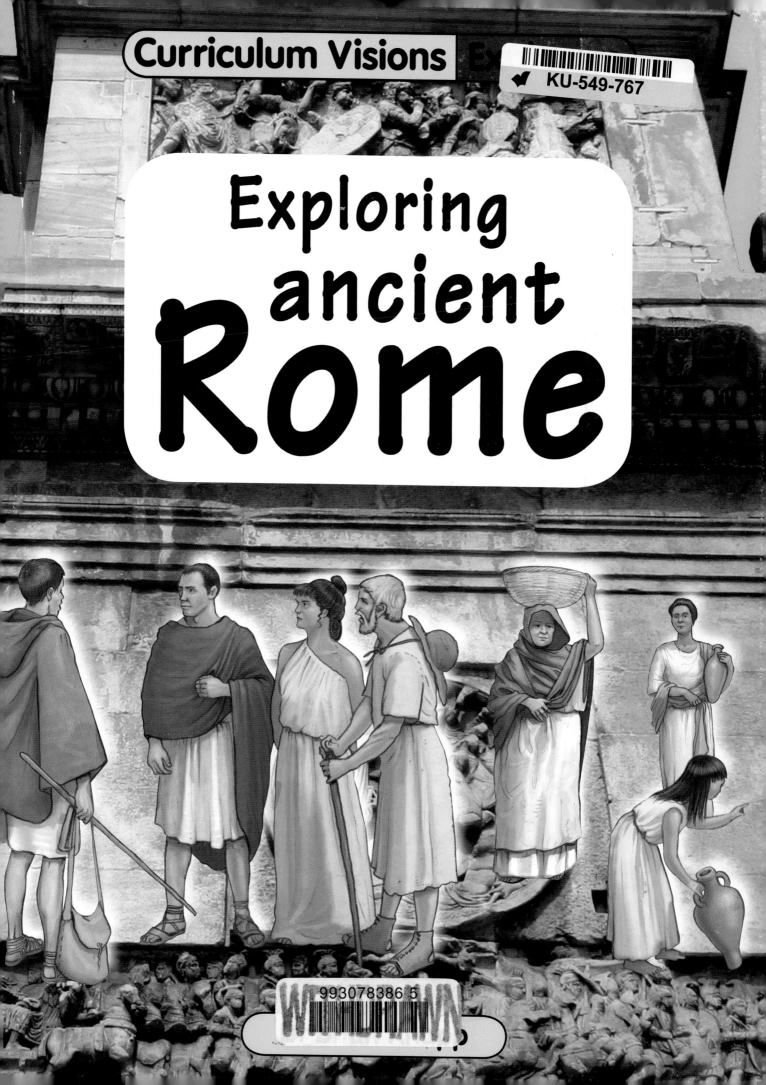

World history

3000 BC	2000 BC	1000 BC

Ancient Egyptians (3000–332 BC)

Ancient Gree

The ruins of many fine buildings from Roman times can still be seen in Rome today. This is a view of the Roman Forum.

Ancient Rome timeline

	The Roman Forum is built	Rome becomes a republic	Gauls attack and set fire to Rome	The first aqueduct	

700 BC	600 BC	500 BC	400 BC	300 BC	200 BC

| Rome founded by King Romulus | The first city walls are built | Early temples are built | New city walls are built | First roads link the cities together | First stone bri over the Tib |

Romans (700BC–476AD)

| 0 | | 1000 AD | | 2000 AD |

00–146BC)

Anglo-Saxons (450–1066)

Vikings (800–1066/1400)

Tudors (1485–1603)

Victorians (1837–1901)

Contents

Look up the **bold** words in the glossary
on page 32 of this book.

Julius Caesar
conquers Gaul

Fire destroys
Rome

Trajan's column
is built

Constantine's
Arch is built

Rome is burned
by barbarians

| 0 | 100 | 200 | 300 | 400 | 500 |

Julius Caesar
assassinated

Ostia, Rome's
port, is built

Walls built that
survive today

Christianity becomes
the main religion

The end of
the empire

Meet the Romans

The ancient Romans lived in the country we now call Italy. They built a vast empire across Europe and the Middle East that lasted for about 1,200 years (from 700 BC to 476 AD). Here are some of them.

Did you know… ?

- Only the Romans in early Roman times wore a toga.
- For most of Roman times men wore tunics which were like long T-shirts.
- The Romans had different tunics for different times of year. In summer they wore linen or cotton tunics to keep them cool. In winter they wore woollen tunics to keep them warm.
- Boys and girls wore a charm around their necks called a bulla. They believed that it kept evil spirits away. Boys took it off when they became citizens and girls took it off when they got married.

Q How are Roman clothes different from the ones people wear today?

Roman gods and temples

The Romans believed that there were gods that looked like humans. They believed that the gods made everything and ruled over every part of their lives. There was, for example, Mars, the god of war, and Minerva, the goddess of wisdom. One god ruled all the others. He was called Jupiter.

The place where the gods were worshipped was the temple. The ruins of many temples can still be seen today.

This is the front of the Pantheon, the most complete temple in Rome.

M·AGRIPPA·L·F·COS·TERTIVM·FECIT

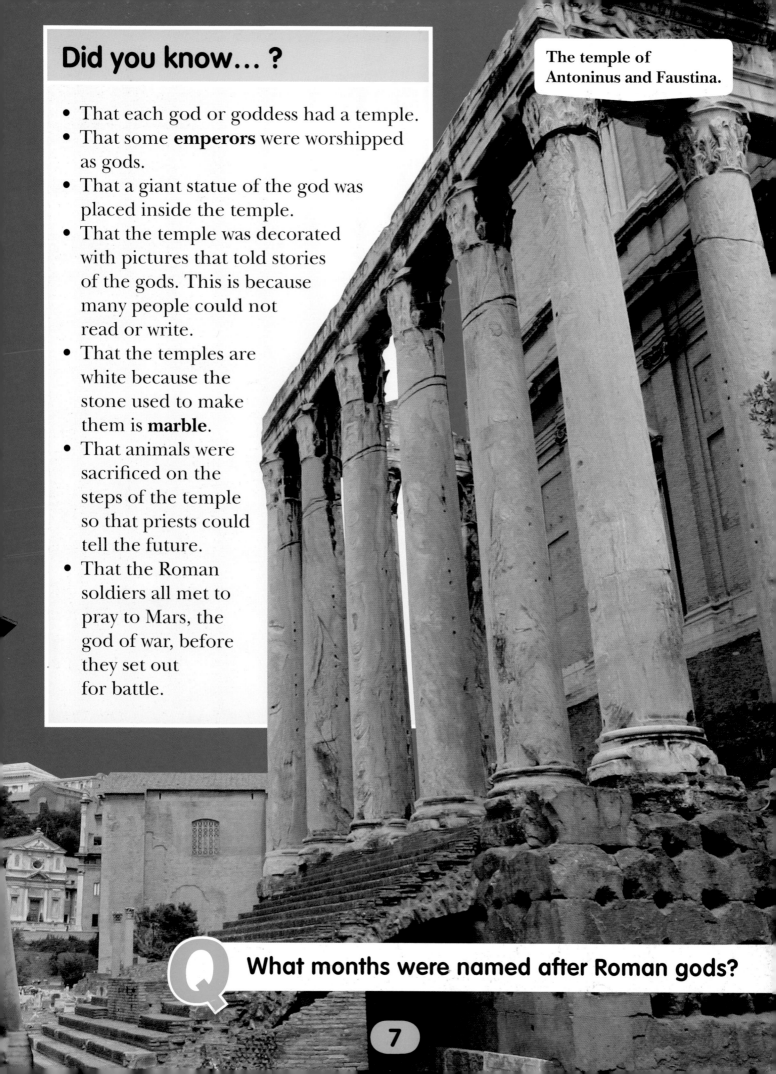

Did you know... ?

- That each god or goddess had a temple.
- That some **emperors** were worshipped as gods.
- That a giant statue of the god was placed inside the temple.
- That the temple was decorated with pictures that told stories of the gods. This is because many people could not read or write.
- That the temples are white because the stone used to make them is **marble**.
- That animals were sacrificed on the steps of the temple so that priests could tell the future.
- That the Roman soldiers all met to pray to Mars, the god of war, before they set out for battle.

The temple of
Antoninus and Faustina.

Q What months were named after Roman gods?

7

The Roman army

The Roman army was used to rule the **provinces** in the **empire**. It was the only army in the world with paid soldiers. This meant that the soldiers were well trained and were the world's best fighters.

Soldiers who were Roman citizens were called legionaries. They wore full armour plating and had big rectangular shields.

Soldiers who were not citizens were called auxiliaries. They had oval shields and had less armour.

The armour worn by a Roman legionary was made of metal plates sewn on to a linen backing so the legionary could move about.

Roman soldiers protected themselves from arrows by holding their shields to form a 'shell'. It was called a testudo, or tortoise.

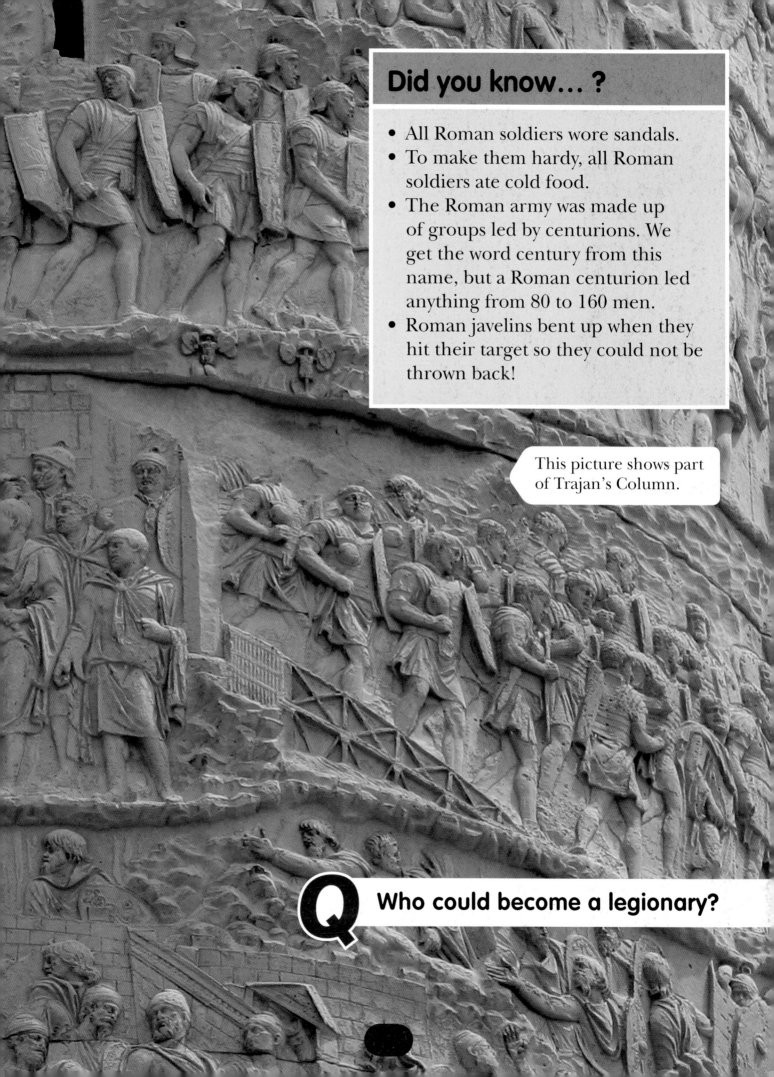

Did you know… ?

- All Roman soldiers wore sandals.
- To make them hardy, all Roman soldiers ate cold food.
- The Roman army was made up of groups led by centurions. We get the word century from this name, but a Roman centurion led anything from 80 to 160 men.
- Roman javelins bent up when they hit their target so they could not be thrown back!

This picture shows part of Trajan's Column.

Q Who could become a legionary?

Famous leaders

Romans were first ruled by a **king**.

Later the kings were overthrown and Romans were ruled by **governors**. But this did not work very well, so generals from the army took over and eventually made themselves emperors.

There were good and bad rulers. Here are some of the most famous.

Julius Caesar was a general. He defeated the French (Gauls) and also invaded Britain (Britannia). He built the Forum in Rome and a new calendar was named after him (Julian calendar). He ruled Rome on his own as a dictator. His enemies stabbed him to death.

Julius Caesar

Augustus was originally called Octavian. He conquered Egypt and added it to the Roman empire. Augustus was the first leader to pay his soldiers a wage.

Augustus

Caligula made things cheaper to buy by getting rid of taxes. This made him very popular. Caligula became mentally ill and insisted that everyone should worship him as a god. In AD 41 he was killed by his own army guard. He was just 29 years old.

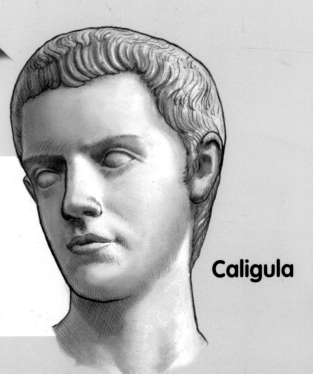

Caligula

Nero

Nero was originally called Lucius Domitius. His mother poisoned the Emperor Claudius, and Nero became emperor. Later Nero killed his mother and his wife, Octavia. In AD 64 Rome was destroyed in a nine-day fire. Nero accused the Christians of having started the fire and had them burned alive. He was just 30 when he ended his own life.

Trajan ruled the people well. The Roman **senate** named him 'optimus', meaning 'the best'. A marble column 30 m high was erected in Rome showing the story of his successful wars (see page 9).

Trajan

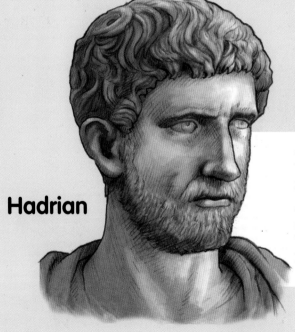

Hadrian

Hadrian was a good leader of the army but he was not able to keep all of the lands that Trajan had won. Hadrian's Wall (begun AD 120) was named after him.

Q **Which of these leaders had months named after them?**

The Forum showing the main temples (T), the basilica or business centre (1), the Tabularium or government record office (2), and an arch built to tell of the success of emperor Septimius Severus (3).

The Forum

Rome was the largest city of the ancient world. Up to a million people may have lived there.

The city centre was called the Roman Forum. There were temples and government buildings in the Forum.

The government buildings were used by people who helped to rule the vast Roman empire. There were open spaces where markets, meetings and parades were held. Some people used to stand in the open spaces and shout out their ideas. They were called orators, and a crowd might gather round them to hear what they had to say.

Q **What do you think the orators talked about?**

The Colosseum

The Colosseum is the largest building that still remains from Roman times. Much of it has been destroyed, so we have to imagine what it was like in Roman times.

Did you know... ?

- The Colosseum is called an amphitheatre. It is something like a modern stadium.
- The Colosseum at Rome could hold 50,000 people. It stands just outside the Roman Forum.

Q What do you think the sound was like?

There used to be seats all around the Colosseum but most are now missing. This small portion has been **restored**.

This is the view you get as you enter the Colosseum. You can see it is made from brick.

This is the inside of the Colosseum. There used to be a floor in the centre (an area called the arena). A small part of it has been replaced, which you can see in the background. Animals and gladiators were kept under the arena floor until it was time for them to fight.

This is the Colosseum at night. Statues used to stand inside each of the arches around the walls. You can get an idea of how tall it is by using the lamp post for scale.

The arena

The Romans liked exciting and violent entertainment. Although they had race tracks for chariot racing (called circuses), theatres and hot baths, their favourite pastime was to go to the amphitheatre to watch fights between people and animals. This is what it might have looked like during Roman times.

This gladiator is using a net to catch his **opponent**, and a trident to stab him.

Did you know…?

- The Colosseum was given this nickname after the colossal (giant) golden statue of Emperor Nero that used to stand next to it.
- The real name of the Colosseum is the Flavian Amphitheatre.
- Thousands of wild animals and people were killed in the arena. Its floor was covered with sand to soak up the blood.

This gladiator has a helmet and visor to protect his head, and a shield to protect his body. He uses the sword to attack his opponent.

Q How would you have felt about watching two gladiators fight to the death?

Homes of the wealthy

Wealthy people lived in a private house. Their rooms were set around a courtyard. There would probably have been a fountain in the middle of the courtyard and the floors would have been tiled with mosaics. The courtyard would have been a cool, shady place to rest in when the weather was hot.

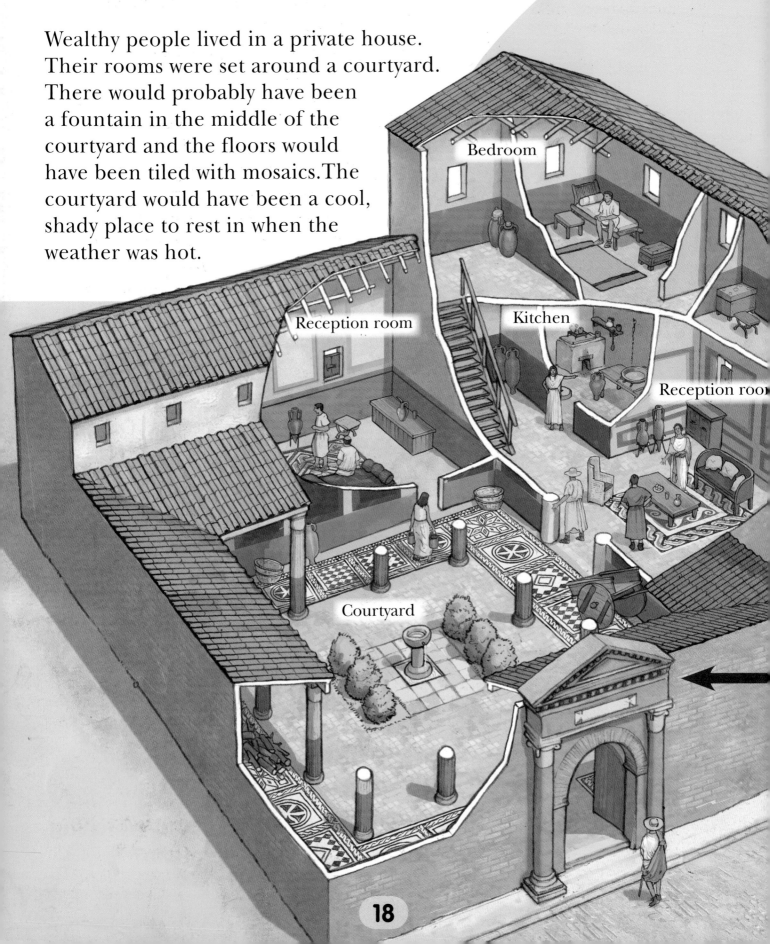

Bedroom

Reception room

Kitchen

Reception room

Courtyard

The home of a wealthy family was called a domus. Its walls were made of brick and it had a tiled roof.

Did you know... ?

- Wealthy Romans were called patricians.
- The children, parents and grandparents of one family lived in a domus.
- The buildings around a courtyard made it private and safe.
- There were paintings on the inside walls of a domus.
- There was little furniture in a domus; just couches for sitting on, low tables and beds.
- A domus had its own toilet and piped water.

Q **What would you see as you made your way from the entrance of the house to the bedroom?**

All the comforts of home

The most wealthy people of Rome could afford all of the comforts of the time.

Clean water was brought into the city by canals. It was then taken through the city in lead pipes to public fountains and also inside the homes of the wealthy.

In winter when it was cool, the homes of wealthy people were heated by warm air that flowed in spaces under the floors and between the walls. The hot air came from fires lit in the basement and stoked by **slaves**.

At night people used oil lamps to light their homes.

Water pipe and fountain.

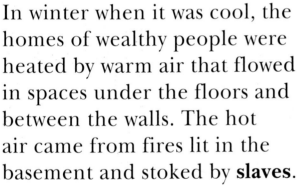

An oil lamp.

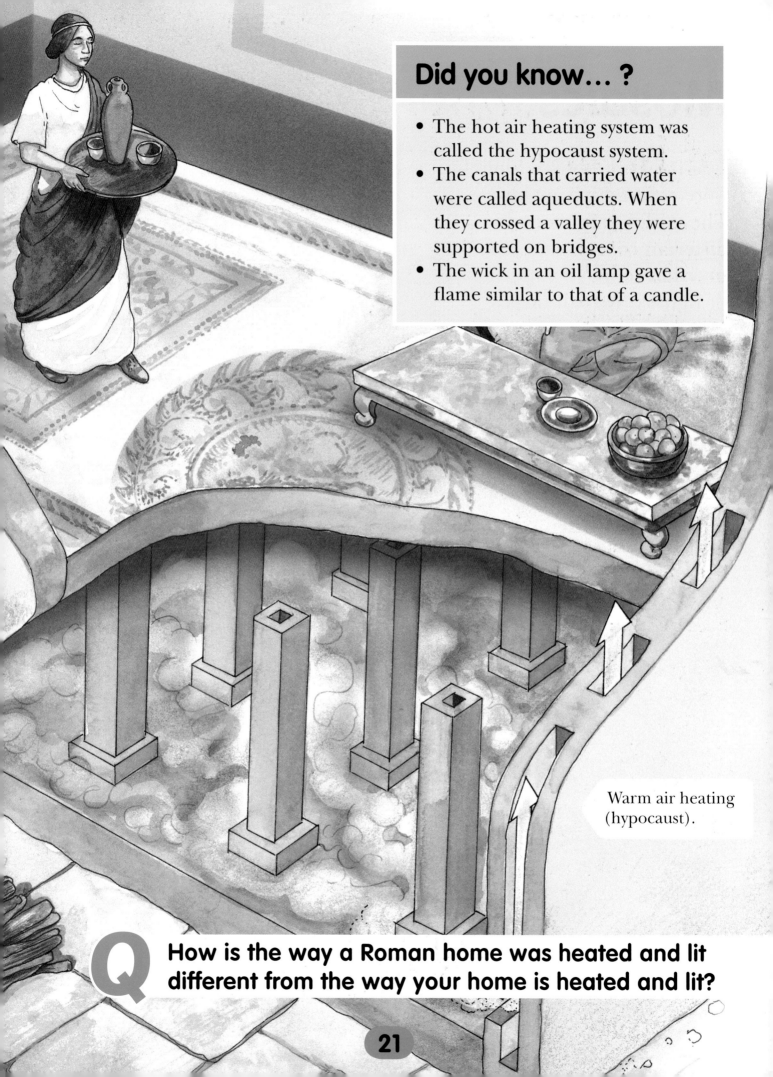

- The hot air heating system was called the hypocaust system.
- The canals that carried water were called aqueducts. When they crossed a valley they were supported on bridges.
- The wick in an oil lamp gave a flame similar to that of a candle.

Warm air heating (hypocaust).

Q **How is the way a Roman home was heated and lit different from the way your home is heated and lit?**

Mosaics

The floors of Roman homes were covered in tiny tiles. These tiles were made in different colours and joined together to make patterns or figures. We call these beautiful floors mosaics.

The tiny tiles of the mosaic were fastened onto the floor with cement.

Did you know... ?

- That the floors of Roman homes were made of tiles because these are cool on the feet and it is hot in Rome in summer.
- A tiled floor is much easier to clean than one made of earth.
- The mosaics could be simple, geometric patterns or scenes from the lives of the gods. The scene in the main picture here shows the sea god, Poseidon.
- That mosaics were not invented by the Romans, but by the ancient Greeks.
- That the little pieces of coloured tile are called tesserae.

Q **What figures can you see in the mosaic on this floor?**

Ordinary homes

Most Romans couldn't afford their own homes and rented an apartment. Apartments were small and had no kitchen and so people had to eat out in fast-food shops. They could buy bread and vegetables with olive oil or lamb and vegetable stew. Some shops were on the ground floor of the apartment blocks the people lived in, so finding something to eat was easy.

The people who lived in the apartments shared a fountain for drinking water.

Did you know... ?

- That an apartment was one or two rooms.
- That an apartment block could be as tall as six storeys high.
- The apartment blocks were built cheaply and often collapsed or burned down.

Roman apartment blocks
were called insulae.

Q Which floor would you have
liked to live on and why?

Everyday life

What was it like living in Rome?

The busiest place was the market. Here you could buy food and clothes, and the pots and dishes you needed.

At home, if you were wealthy, you would have a slave bring your food. You would eat it lying on your side on a couch.

At a busy marketplace people, donkeys and carts carried in the goods to be sold.

Dinner in a wealthy home.

Did you know… ?

- That the Roman market was called an **agora**.
- That wine, oils and other liquids were kept in long pointed jars called amphorae. Any solids settled out in the pointed end.
- That few women were to be seen in the market because it was thought that a woman's place was in charge of the home.
- Fashionable crockery came from the south of France. It was called Samian ware.

Q How did people carry their amphorae?

Roads

The Romans were famous for the roads they built. All of the city roads were paved with stone blocks, as were the roads connecting cities all over the empire. Parts of the Forum were paved with marble.

Did you know... ?

- That Roman roads were arched up so that water would flow off them.
- That Roman roads between cities were straight.
- That most Roman roads between cities were built by the army.
- That the Roman name for a road is via (Latin).
- That the straight roads allowed the army to travel quickly to defend the empire.

Here the main road with its paving stones crosses the middle of a Forum paved with marble slabs.

Q What would it have been like to march in wet weather along a road that was not paved?

Try these...

Play Knucklebones

Roman children played a game called Knucklebones. They used sheep ankle bones but you can make them from Plasticine or self-hardening clay.

Make five knucklebones in the following way:

- Cut up the Plasticine or clay into a lump 1.5 cm long, 1 cm wide and 1 cm high. Make it knobbly as the picture shows.

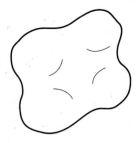

- Make holes on the six sides like the spots on dice.
- Place the knucklebones in the palm of your hand, throw them up and see how many you can catch on the back of your hand.
- Write down the number of holes on the tops of the knucklebones. Challenge a friend to beat you.

Assemble broken pottery

Much of what we know about the Romans comes from the broken remains of the things they left behind. Archaeologists carefully dig out the remains and put them back together to see how they looked in Roman times. Set an archaeological challenge for a friend in the following way:

- Make a drawing of an amphora about 10 cm high on a piece of card.
- Cut it up into bits and place it in a saucer of sand.
- Challenge your friend to find all the pieces carefully and stick them back together.

Use Roman numbers

The Romans used different symbols for their numbers to the ones we use today. Here they are:

1	2	3	4	5	6	7
I	II	III	IV	V	VI	VII
8	9	10	50	100	500	1000
VIII	IX	X	L	C	D	M

- Write the following in Roman numerals – your age, your house number, the year, and other measurements like the width of this page.

Speak Latin

The Romans spoke in a language called Latin. Here are some Latin words and phrases to try with your friends. Can you understand each other?

English	Latin
Hello	salve
What is your name?	quod nomen tibi est?
My name is…	mihi nomen est…
Where do you live?	ubi habitas?
I live in	habito
Goodbye	vale

Make a writing tablet

- Make a border round a piece of card as the picture shows:

- Rub a wax crayon on the large space inside the border. Use a piece of wood with a point on it to scratch letters in the wax. Write the letters of the Roman alphabet shown here:

A B C D E F G
H I K L M N O
P Q R S T V X Z

- Note that I and J are both written as I and V and U are both written as V. The alphabet does not have a W or a Y.

Counting words

Lots of our words come from Latin.

uni = one   bi = two
tri = three   cent = hundred

Can you find any words that begin with these?

Glossary

agora Latin (Roman) word for a marketplace.

emperor A leader who rules an empire.

empire A huge area of land made up from different countries which all have one ruler or leader.

governor A person who is voted to be leader by important people in a country.

king A man in the leading family in a country, called the royal family, who becomes leader of that country.

marble A type of white rock, which can be cut to have smooth, shiny surfaces.

opponent A person who sets themselves against another person, such as one fighter opposing or fighting against another.

provinces Different parts of an empire which might be ruled in slightly different ways from the others. For example, they have different governors.

restored Repaired to make it look as it did when it was first made.

senate A group of people who carry out the government of a country.

slaves People who were owned by other people.

Index

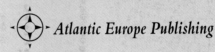

Curriculum Visions

Curriculum Visions is a registered trademark of Atlantic Europe Publishing Company Ltd.

Atlantic Europe Publishing

Curriculum Visions Explorers
This series provides straightforward introductions to key worlds and ideas.

You might also be interested in
'The Romans in Britain'. There is a Teacher's Guide to match 'The Romans in Britain'. Additional notes in PDF format are also available from the publisher to support 'Exploring ancient Rome'. All of these products are suitable for KS2.

Dedicated Web Site
Watch movies, see many more pictures and read much more in detail about the Romans at:
www.curriculumvisions.com
(Professional Zone: subscription required)

First published in 2007 by Atlantic Europe Publishing Company Ltd
Copyright © 2007 Earthscape

Author
Brian Knapp, BSc, PhD

Consulting Editor and Contributor
Peter Riley, BSc, C Biol, MI Biol, PGCE
(material on pages 30–31 is based on the *Curriculum Visions' The Romans in Britain Teacher's Guide* authored by Peter Riley)

Educational Consultants
JM Smith (former Deputy Head of Wellfield School, Burnley, Lancashire); the Librarians of Hertfordshire School Library Service

Senior Designer
Adele Humphries, BA

Editor
Gillian Gatehouse

Photographs
The Earthscape Picture Library, except *Colonia Ostiensis* p29.

Illustrations
Mark Stacey

Designed and produced by
Earthscape

Printed in China by
WKT Company Ltd

Exploring ancient Rome – *Curriculum Visions*
A CIP record for this book is available from the British Library
ISBN 978 1 86214 203 9